European Forum of Sign Language Interpreters

*Learning Outcomes for Graduates of a Three Year Sign Language Interpreting Training Programme*

 Lifelong Learning Programme

This project has been funded with support from the European Commission. This publication reflects the views only of the author, and the Commission cannot be held responsible for any use which may be made of the information contained therein.

ISBN: 9789081306553

© European Forum of Sign Language Interpreters, 2013

**Edited by**: efsli

**Cover design by**: Liivi Hollman

**Cover photos**: efsli. efsli working seminars: Utrecht (November 2011), Hamburg (March 2012) and Dublin (February 2013)

**Readers**: Lourdes Calle Alberdi, Lorraine Leeson, Marinella Salami

**Printed by**: *Createspace*

No part of this publication may be produced, stored in a retrieval system or transmitted in any form or any means (electronic, photocopying, recording or otherwise), without the prior written permission of the publisher.

Whenever you publish an article/paper or present results based on or referring to the efsli learning outcomes data, please include the following acknowledgement or an appropriate equivalent:

"We wish to thank the European Forum of Sign Language Interpreters (efsli) for providing the data used in this paper. The European Forum of Sign Language Interpreters (efsli) is a not-for-profit ONG representing sign language interpreters across Europe – www.efsli.org"

The European Forum of Sign Language Interpreters (efsli) is a not-for-profit NGO consisting of national associations of sign language interpreters. It is the only organisation representing sign language interpreters at a European level, comprising a very wide network of sign language interpreters and organisations. efsli fosters a vision of high European-wide standards of sign language interpreting services which enable interpreters to fulfill their work in a professional manner.

Being a forum where good practices and expertise are shared between all stakeholders in the field of sign language interpreting, efsli aims to constantly enhance the status of the profession through higher standards of continuing education, professional recognition and adequate working conditions.

The present publication is an example of efsli's contribution to define this process of quality improvement.

# Table of contents

1. Foreword — 6
2. Acknowledgments — 9
3. Introduction — 15
4. Prologue — 19
5. Domain of knowledge: Signed Language/s & Sign Linguistics — 26
6. Domain of Knowledge: Spoken and/or Written Languages — 29
7. Domain of knowledge: Interpreting — 31
8. Domain of knowledge: Deaf Communities and Deaf Culture — 35
9. Domain of knowledge: Ethics and Decision Making — 38
10. Domain of knowledge: Interpreting for Specific Populations — 40
11. Domain of knowledge: Interpreting in Specific Settings — 44
12. Domain of knowledge: Professional knowledge — 47
13. Glossary — 49
14. References — 59

# Foreword

*Marinella Salami, efsli president*

In 1994 the European Forum of Sign Language Interpreters (efsli) published a slim, bilingual (English and German) volume with a dark, iridescent blue cover bearing the title "Blueprint 2000". During that year – 1994 – the European Union and the European Union of the Deaf (EUD) funded a special workshop, orgnised by efsli in cooporation with Scottish Association of Sign Language interpreters (SASLI), where it was agreed that 2000 was the year by which each country within Europe had to aspire to achieve a particular set of "ideal standards". The final document (with the iridescent blue cover) with more detailed recommendations was then prepared. I read through these recommendations again just recently; and smiled. It was a smile of appreciation and, indeed, praise. Just like good marathon runners crossing the finishing line, many of the efsli member countries successfully met the agreed targets by the 2000 deadline.

Many years have passed since the publication of that booklet and the European social context for sign language interpreters has changed considerably. Boundaries have been expanded, concepts refined and targets have been lifted to even higher levels of achievement. efsli has moved on too since that deadline; building its character and establishing a broader and stronger European profile. Education and training for sign language interpreters - based on shared, common standards - was one of the three main concepts discussed by efsli delegates in 1994 and this publication is an evolution of that original concept, taking it

## foreword

even further than then imagined.

The results of our project on "Learning Outcomes for Graduates of a Three Year Sign Language Interpreting Training Programme" mark a milestone in the construction of a united Europe while preserving language and cultural diversity, as well as social and educational traditions. They also perfectly match the idea behind the *free movement of people* principle: equal training opportunities for sign language interpreters and quality services for Deaf citizens across the entire Union. It is of crucial importance to guarantee Deaf EU citizens the possibility of moving to any EU country and benefitting from the same interpreting services, in terms of quality, in any field of life as they could expect in their home country (or anywhere else in the EU). This document will surely be remembered as an historic breakthrough in the years to come. You will find a description of the project phases in the *Introduction*, while an explanatory account of the guiding principles is given in the *Prologue*.

On a more personal note, I would like to acknowledge a colleague and dear friend of mine, Maya de Wit, former efsli president, for her valuable input in starting the learning outcomes process and for devoting her precious time to help complete the initial stages of this project. I had the privilege of working with her on the efsli Board. We both saw the project take shape and produce its first, exciting results. I found it especially rewarding that we could work together and share this experience. This publication is actually the result of years of

## *foreword*

fruitful cooperation and teamwork of many different people all over Europe, excellently coordinated by Lourdes Calle Alberdi, the efsli project coordinator. Our gratitude to them is expressed in the "Acknowledgements Section" in the pages that follow. All of our efforts would have been in vain had it not been for their their generous contributions.

While I'm writing this foreword, the world is celebrating the fiftieth anniversary of Martin Luther King's "I have a dream" speech. There are still so many disparities at different levels within our societies. Equality of access and services for linguistic and cultural minorities are no exception.

We still have a dream. Our minds have already turned to future challenges. This document is intended as just a starting point for future research and discussion within both the sign language interpreting and Deaf communities; one that, we hope, will have positive repercussions for training programmes and professional associations alike.

Indeed, Dr King's words still echo today:

> "We cannot walk alone. And as we walk, we must make the pledge that we shall always march ahead. We cannot turn back".

# Acknowledgements

*From the efsli team*

This work on learning outcomes would have not been possible without the support and the encouragement of so many people in so many ways, who we would like to acknowledge in this section.

We would like to thank all the members and partners of efsli for their active cooperation in constructing each step of the learning outcomes project, and all the participants and hosts of the three efsli working seminars for their valued contributions and for making each seminar a memorable experience. In particular, our heartfelt thanks go to Beppie van den Bogaerde (Institute for Sign Language and Deaf Studies, Hogeschool Utrecht, Netherlands), Christian Rathmann (Institut für Deutsche Gebärdensprache und Kommunikation Gehörloser, Universität Hamburg, Germany) and Lorraine Leeson (Centre for Deaf Studies, School of Linguistics, Speech and Communication Science, Trinity College Dublin, Ireland) along with their respective teams of professionals and volunteers for the great effort they made in organising the three working seminars with us.

We are also deeply grateful to the thirty-three sign language interpreting training programmes across Europe that took part in our initial survey and continued to contribute to any follow-up of this project. Their generous support and expertise stimulated a high-level academic discussion and helped us pursue our path of development:

- BA Transkulturelle Kommunikation (Karl-Franzens-

## acknowledgements

Universität Graz, Austria);

- MA Dolmetschen (Karl-Franzens-Universität Graz, Austria);
- Fachausbildung Gebärdensprachdolmetschen (GESDO, Linz, Austria);
- Achtung Fertig Los (ÖGSDV, Austria);
- Graduaat Tolk Vlaamse Gebarentaal (VSPW Ghent, Belgium);
- Graduaat Tolk Vlaamse Gebarentaal (CVO Crescendo, Mechelen, Belgium);
- Bachelor in de Toegepaste Taalkunde (Lessius University College, Antwerp, Belgium);
- Master in het Tolken (Lessius University College, Antwerp, Belgium), Postgraduaat conferentietolken (Lessius University College, Antwerp, Belgium);
- Komplexní vzdělávací systému pro tlumočníky českého znakového jazyka (Deaf Institute for Specialized Education, Prague, Czech Republic);
- Forsøgsuddannelse til tegnsprogstolk (Professionshøjskolen UCC, Copenhagen, Denmark);
- Eesti Viipekeele Tõlk (University of Tartu, Tallinn, Estonia);
- Viittomakielentulkin koulutusohjelma (Diaconia University of Applied Sciences, Turku, Finland);

*acknowledgements*

- Viittomakielentulkki AMK (HUMAK University of Applied Sciences, Kuopio and Helsinki, Finland);

- Master d'interprétation Français/LSF, LSF/Français (University Paris 3, France);

- Master professionnel interprétariat en langue des signes (University Paris 8, France);

- Master sciences du langage: Interprétariat Langue des Signes Française / Français (University Lille 3, France);

- Studiengang Gebaerdensprachdolmetschen (University of Applied Sciences, Zwickau, Germany), BA Gebärdensprachdolmetschen (Hamburg University, Germany);

- MA Gebärdensprachdolmetschen, (Hamburg University, Germany);

- Akademische Weiterbildung für taube Gebärdensprachdolmetscher (Hamburg University, Germany);

- Bachelor in Deaf studies (Trinity College Dublin, Ireland);

- Teoria e tecniche di traduzione e interpretazione italiano / lingua dei segni italiana- LIS (Ca'Foscari University, Venice, Italy);

- Gestų kalba (Vilniaus kolegija/University of Applied Sciences, Lithuania);

- Bachelor i tegnspråk og tolking (Sør-Trøndelag University College, Trondheim, Norway);

## *acknowledgements*

- Bachelor i tegnspråk og tolking (Oslo & Akershus University College, Norway);

- Bachelor i tegnspråk og tolking, (Bergen University College, Norway);

- Polska studia podyplomowe język migowy (University of Warsaw, Poland);

- Pripravljalni program za pridobitev poklica tolmač slovenskega znakovnega jezika (Association of Slovene Sign Language Interpreters, Ljubljana, Slovenia);

- Ciclo formativo de grado superior en interpretación de lengua de signos (Ministry of Education, Spain);

- Master oficial en docencia e interpretación de lenguas de señas (Valladolid University, Spain);

- Grado en Traducción e Interpretación (Pompeu Fabra University, Spain):

- Teckenspråks- och dövblindtolkutbildning vid Södertörns folkhögskola - Gamla stan (Södertörns folkhögskola - Gamla stan, Stockholm, Sweden);

Finally, and above all, we owe a debt of gratitude to the efsli Committee of Experts (eCE), chaired by Professor Lorraine Leeson, for their valuable advice, untiring support and guidance throughout this two-year journey. The members of this group of dedicated professionals committed themselves and generously spent their time working on this excellent and unique docu-

*acknowledgements*

ment. Therefore, we would like to take this opportunity to extend our sincere gratitude and appreciation to all of them for kindly sharing their expertise and knowledge. We proudly thank them for believing in our goal, for their perseverance and passion:

- Professor Lorraine Leeson, Trinity College Dublin (Ireland)
- Mr. Barry-Alan Davey (UK)
- Ms. Sarah Bown, University of Wolverhampton (UK)
- Ms. Ebru Diriker, Bogazici University (Turkey) and University of Manchester (UK)
- Mr. Zane Hema (Australia)
- Mr. Robert Lee, University of Central Lancashire (UK)
- Mr. Peter Llewellyn-Jones, University of Leeds (UK)
- Professor Christian Rathmann, University of Hamburg (Germany)
- Ms. Camilla Warnicke, University of Örebro (Sweden)

In July 2013, Professor Jemina Napier, Heriot Watt University (Scotland), also joined the Committee and gave her valuable academic input for the preparation of this document.

This project was supported by the Operating Grant awarded to efsli by the European Commission's Lifelong Learning Pro-

## acknowledgements

gramme (LLP) under a three-year grant agreement (2011-2013). We gratefully acknowledge their financial support.

Once again, thank you all!

# Introduction

*Lourdes Calle Alberdi, efsli project coordinator*

This publication is the result of an enriching two-year process, in which over one hundred sign language interpreters and trainers from across Europe collaborated with efsli in coming to an agreement on a European learning outcomes proposal for sign language interpreters.

The first step of this process took place in October, 2011 when a comprehensive survey was sent to more than fifty sign language interpreter training programmes in Europe. The purpose of this questionnaire was to gather all the information available in order to have an overview of sign language interpreter education to date. It included questions on several aspects of the training programmes, such as requirements for student access, input on curriculum and trainers, etc. At this early stage, eighteen training programmes responded. Responses increased to twenty -seven in February, 2012, and to thirty-three in May, 2012. With the information collected, efsli wrote the report, *Sign Language Interpreter Training Programmes-draft* which was updated in March 2012 and again in September 2013 including all current responses. This document provided the foundation for the discussion in the I efsli working seminar, *Towards a Standard Curriculum for Sign Language Interpreters Across Europe* (Utrecht, Netherlands, November, 2011). The seminar focused on best practices

## introduction

in sign language interpreter teaching. Interpreters and trainers engaged in twelve workshops in which they discussed the report findings and the challenges faced by trainers throughout Europe.

In order to launch the second phase of this process, which started in early 2012, efsli presented a first "Learning Outcomes" draft. This was presented in the II efsli working seminar called *Towards a Standard Curriculum for Sign Language Interpreters across Europe: Coming to an agreement on learning outcomes and curriculum content.* (Hamburg, Germany, March 2012). The findings of the Utrecht workshops as well as the updated report on sign language interpreting training programmes (March 2012) were both essential ingredients for the preparation of this document. This working document was organised into domains of knowledge, and provided the core material for the discussion in the nine workshops that took place in Hamburg. Once again, interpreters and trainers from across Europe revised and discussed this working document, making proposals on how to improve it. Although rich discussions took place at these workshops, participants agreed that there was further need for revision of the proposal. Therefore, it was decided to open an online platform with which to continue the discussions. This platform was launched in October 2012. Through the online forums, participants debated the Learning Outcomes draft updated during the Hamburg workshops. An updated version of the Learning Outcomes pro-

*introduction*

posal was drafted which included comments and amendments proposed in the forums.

The third phase, which occurred between November 2012 and July 2013, consisted of the revision of the document by the efsli Committee of Experts (eCE), chaired by Professor Lorraine Leeson ,Trinity College Dublin, Ireland. The eCE undertook a detailed revision of the proposal. The result of this review, entitled *Learning Outcomes for Graduates of a Three Year Interpreting Programme*-draft, was presented at the III efsli working seminar, *Quality Assessment —A European Model for Sign Language Interpreter Education and Training* (Dublin, Ireland, February 2013). This seminar had a dual objective: on the one hand, to discuss assessment methods and instruments for sign language interpreter education, an on the other hand, to present the document revised by the eCE. This was the last time feedback was collected before publishing a final version. The result of this process is the present document.

In conclusion, this has been both a collaborative and inclusive process in which diverse experiences and expertise were shared and discussed. Sign language interpreters and trainers from twenty-two different countries participated and gave their input on what they considered the minimum skills set a sign language interpreter student should acquire in order to become a gradu-

*introduction*

---

ate interpreter. We expect this publication to be groundbreaking in establishing a standard for both the sign language interpreter and the Deaf communities across Europe. We consider it a significant accomplishment on the part of efsli. We hope this is just the beginning of further endeavours that embrace collaboration and a mutual understanding among sign language interpreters across Europe.

# Prologue

*Prof. Lorraine Leeson, chair of the efsli Committee of Experts (eCE)*

The following comments are intended to provide an overview of some of the guiding principles that were applied in the preparation of these revised documents.

The primary data source that we have drawn on is the set of competencies drawn up as a result of efsli workshops in preparing the "Summary Goals" for each domain of knowledge. This current set of Learning Outcomes presents a streamlined version of those previously circulated, following principles of best practice for the creation of documents like this. In preparing this document, our primary goal is that the learning outcomes apply to interpreters across the board, regardless of hearing status. Thus, except in the case of the domain of knowledge that looks at spoken language, all learning outcomes outline desirable threshold competencies for graduate interpreters in our field, whether they work between two signed languages, between signed and spoken languages, or between written forms of language and a signed language/s.

Our brief was to prepare a document that outlined the learning outcomes that graduates of a three year university-based sign language interpreter training programme would be expected to attain. It is essential to remember that learning outcomes for each domain of competency listed here are written at the threshold level of a pass – that is, they are considered to be minimal level competencies for entry to the profession. However, in general terms, programme outcomes for degree courses are written for a typical or average student and they can be more

## prologue

aspirational. In either case though, the most suitable learning outcomes are considered to be those which are most honest, precise and informative (Scattergood, 2008). In preparing this document, we aimed for Scattergood's goal of presenting precise, informative, and honest (vis-à-vis fitness to practice goals) – and indeed, assessable – competencies based on efsli's wide-ranging consultation with interpreter trainers.

Each learning outcome must be assessable. While it is not necessary to individually and independently assess each learning outcome, over the course of a programme, individual clusters of learning outcomes should be examined as part of formative or summative assessment processes.

In preparing this document, we predicate the threshold learning outcomes for language domains on the following notional estimations: that students are following a course of study that is three years in duration and that the majority of students have no signed language at entry. We assume approximately six hours of face-to-face teaching in the national/regional sign language a week. Assuming an average academic year that comprises 24 weeks of classes, this gives us a total of approximately 432 hours of formal instruction across the life of a three-year degree programme. For our purposes we are assuming that students will complete somewhere in the region of four hours of self-study for a week, which gives us an aggregate of 288 hours of additional learning over the three years. Collectively, this suggests that an average student taking a three-year degree programme will have completed somewhere in the region of 720 hours of signed language study as part of their undergraduate training. This is an important estimation when it comes to considering language development and what we should expect as minimal language and interpreting proficiency outcomes on completion of training, though we fully appreciate that actual hours of face to face teaching will differ across institutions and countries. We also draw on the following rough estimation of input required to achieve certain threshold levels of CEFR aligned second language competency from ALTE, the Association of Language Testers in Europe, (Van den Bogaerde and Oyserman 2011) and we acknowledge that the time required to achieve a certain threshold of competency may differ across particular groups:

| A1 | Approx. 90 to 100 hours    | Max. 100 hours  |
|----|----------------------------|-----------------|
| A2 | Approx. 180 to 200 hours   | Max. 300 hours  |
| B1 | Approx. 350 to 400 hours   | Max. 700 hours  |
| B2 | Approx. 500 to 600 hours   | Max. 1300 hours |
| C1 | Approx. 700 to 800 hours   | Max. 2100 hours |
| C2 | Approx. 1000 to 1200 hours | Max. 3300 hours |

Given all of this, the learning outcomes for signed language and interpreting domains of knowledge are mapped onto CEFR level CI for receptive language skills and B2 for productive language skills. Again, we emphasise that these are the minimum threshold levels for a pass grade and this does not mean that some students will not attain higher levels of proficiency. The goal here is

# *prologue*

to present threshold level descriptors.

We also emphasise that our perspective is that signed language interpreting curricula should be delivered by teams of Deaf and hearing academics and practitioners working collaboratively. Indeed, we can say that for some domains of knowledge, an "insider" Deaf perspective is a very powerful catalyst for facilitating student learning, and nothing can replace access to highly competent L1 usage in the target languages which students will work with. Furthermore, we see it as crucial that student signed language interpreters have the opportunity to engage with Deaf communities during their training period, not only from the academic point of view (by reading and analysing the literature on Deaf community, Deaf culture, etc.). Service learning should be built into training programmes, facilitating and encouraging connections to and engagement with Deaf communities. This provides students with an opportunity to develop authentic links to the Deaf community and offers insight into their position within the community they will work with and serve as graduates. It also gives Deaf community members the opportunity to get to know potential future interpreters over time, allowing for the building up of rapport and trust.

In addition, we recommend that work placement modules be included into curricula. The embedding of a number of placement periods over the life of an interpreter training programme offers staged supervised authentic encounters for students. Such opportunities to meet, observe and (in the later stages) work alongside professional interpreters in practice cannot be under-

## prologue

estimated in terms of motivation for students and in terms of gaining real world experience to bring to bear to counterbalance their academic understanding of the field. To embed several placement periods along the training programme, with different length and aims according to the training stage they are in, will assure an adequate preparation for their future professional practice.

It is essential to note that this is a notional document: we know that a one size fits all approach is not desirable or appropriate, as national and local policy, tradition, resources, and infrastructures differ significantly. For example, some programmes which are three years in duration offer training to interpreters who work with several languages. In this tradition, a three-year programme prepares interpreters to work consecutively, so the learning outcomes listed here for the simultaneous interpreting will clearly not apply. In such programmes simultaneous interpreting is taught at postgraduate level. In other places, there is still only ad hoc interpreter training available. Thus, this document may serve at present as a reference framework which represents the minimal threshold competencies that interpreter trainers and practitioners from across Europe believe are required for practice.


On behalf of the efsli Committee of Experts,

Prof. Lorraine Leeson

Chair, efsli Committee of Experts (eCE)

*prologue*

Members of the efsli Committee of Experts:

- Professor Lorraine Leeson, Trinity College Dublin (Ireland) (Chair)
- Mr. Barry Allan Davey (UK)
- Ms. Sarah Bown, University of Wolverhampton (UK)
- Ms. Ebru Diriker, Bogazici University (Turkey) and University of Manchester (UK)
- Mr. Zane Hema (Australia)
- Mr. Robert Lee, University of Central Lancashire (UK)
- Mr. Peter Llewellyn-Jones, University of Leeds (UK)
- Professor Jemina Napier, Heriot Watt University (Scotland). In the eCE since 2013.
- Professor Christian Rathmann, University of Hamburg (Germany)
- Ms. Camilla Warnicke, University of Örebro (Sweden)

*Learning Outcomes for Graduates of a Three Year Sign Language Interpreting Training Programme*

# Domains of knowledge

# Signed language/s and sign linguistics

*Domain of knowledge 1*

## Summary goal:

*A graduate should demonstrate communicative competence and flexibility in sign language by effectively communicating in a variety of routine personal and professional situations with native and non-native speakers of varying ages, gender, education and socio-economic status*

## Learning outcomes:

On successful completion of the course, graduates should be able to:

### Sign Linguistics:

1. Describe the central notions and analytical methods of major areas of general and applied linguistics, namely phonological, morphological, syntactic and lexical structures, sociolinguistic aspects of language, discourse/text analysis, and semantic and pragmatic features of language.

2. Demonstrate capacity to gloss and appraise a segment of signed data.

### Signed Language/s:

3. Demonstrate competent receptive and productive use of fingerspelling.

## signed language/s and sign linguistics

4. Produce idiomatically appropriate and genre specific utterances in their working signed language/s.

5. Effectively communicate in a variety of routine personal and professional situations with native and non-native speakers of varying ages, gender, education, socio-economic status.

6. Present clear, detailed descriptions on a wide range of subjects.

7. Develop a clear argument, expanding and supporting his/her points of view at some length with subsidiary points and relevant examples.

8. Produce clear, coherent and well expressed signed texts utilising a range of registers, styles, technical terms and select alternative strategies such as paraphrasing in accordance with the context of use, whilst observing conventions of specific text genres, including formal settings and functions.

9. Handle turn-taking and interactions effectively.

10. Demonstrate capacity to follow extended signing even when it is not clearly structured and when relationships are only implied and not signalled explicitly.

11. Demonstrate capacity to follow long and complex discourse, appreciating distinctions of style and can decipher complex technical information.

*signed language/s and sign linguistics*

12. Demonstrate capacity to follow complex interactions between third parties in-group discussion and debate, even on abstract, complex and unfamiliar topics.

13. Analyse the effectiveness of sign language performance generated by self and peers by applying contemporary theories of performance assessment and peer review.

# Spoken and/or written languages

*Domain of knowledge 2*

## Summary goal:

*A graduate should demonstrate high levels of proficiency and flexibility in the reception and production of the spoken and written language by effectively communicating in a wide range of situations, with speakers of various ages and backgrounds whilst demonstrating cultural and intercultural awareness and sensitivity.*

## Learning outcomes:

On successful completion of the course, graduates should be able to:

1. Describe frames/ schemas/scripts and their relevance to interpreting/ translational processes.

2. Recognise and produce forms and functions of spoken and/or written language use across a broad range of genres.

3. Manage the inter/intra situational factors that impact upon the reception and production of spoken/written texts, selecting appropriate strategies when required.

*spoken and/or written languages*

---

4. Define the range of cultural and social dimensions within language use (connotations of words, text norms, forms of politeness, etc.)

5. Identify, describe and demonstrate capacity to deal with translational and interactional challenges

6. Demonstrate capacity to follow spoken and/or written language texts that contain linguistic variation, different text genres and cultural backgrounds.

7. Produce coherent and well expressed spoken texts utilising a range of registers, styles, technical terms and select alternative strategies such as paraphrasing in accordance with the context of use, whilst adjusting the volume as appropriate to the environment and by observing conventions of specific text genres, including formal settings and functions.

8. Analyse written texts in preparation for translation/interpretation, incorporating annotations that justify translation decisions.

9. Produce clear, coherent and well expressed written texts utilising a range of registers, styles, technical terms and select alternative strategies such as paraphrasing in accordance with the context of use, whilst observing conventions of specific text genres, including formal settings and functions.

# Interpreting

*Domain of knowledge 3*

## Summary goal:

The graduate should demonstrate capacity to interpret proficiently and effectively in consecutive and simultaneous modes. They should be able to prepare for an assignment, draw on the literature in the interpreting field and in the domains in which they will work, and apply this to their work as independent interpreters, as members of an interpreting team, and as members of the interpreting profession. This entails that a graduate interpreter demonstrates capacity to manage the social factors that influence an interpreter's activities (e.g. Turn-taking, overlapping turns, power relations, expectations and requirements, etc.) in a non-dominating manner and that they are able to explain the interpreting process and their scope of practice to consumers. Finally, graduate interpreters should demonstrate collegiality by showing respect and courtesy to colleagues, consumers and employers, and by taking responsibility for the quality of their work.

*interpreting*

## Learning outcomes:

On successful completion of the course, graduates should be able to:

1. Critically discuss and apply the main concepts, models, and methodological approaches in the field of Interpreting Studies, for example Demand and Control Schema, the Efforts Model, Miscue Analysis and Skopos Theory.

2. Describe in detail the notion of "equivalence" at word level, clause level, sentence level, grammatical level and discourse level.

3. Identify and evaluate social factors that influence an interpreter's activities (such as turn-taking, overlapping turns, power relations).

4. Evaluate the impact that cultural difference plays in interpreted events.

5. Carry out an accurate analysis of an interpreting assignment, drawing on Interpreting Studies literature to inform assessment.

6. Select the most appropriate interpreting mode in specific contexts, taking account of the function and the context of the event.

7. Apply common interpreting strategies in practice, including management of turn-taking.

8. Apply different modes of interpreting in practice including simultaneous, consecutive, written translation and sight interpreting.

9. Apply appropriate interpreting and translating strategies when dealing with incongruence between language pairs.

10. Efficiently manage and repair communication in interpreting settings using a range of interpreting techniques.

11. Describe and demonstrate appropriate preparation techniques.

12. Generate a working glossary of terms/concepts for common interpreting/translating environments.

13. Write effective notes during consecutive interpreting, as required.

14. Interpret prepared and unprepared texts.

15. Compose target language interpretations/translations that are culturally appropriate.

16. Work effectively as part of an interpreting/translating team.

*interpreting*

17. Outline the range of strategies and techniques that can be drawn on when working as part of an interpreting/translating team, including relay interpreting.

18. Utilise technology used in the sign language interpreting and translation field.

19. Adjust linguistic output to maximise target language efficacy where new technologies are used including remote interpreting services and video relay interpreting.

20. Devise a personalised Continuous Professional Development profile and plan.

# Deaf Communities and Deaf Culture

*Domain of knowledge 4*

## Summary goal:

*A graduate should apply their knowledge of Deaf Studies literature to their work as an interpreter/translator. For example, they should have the capacity to embed key Deaf cultural traditions, values and norms within their approach to interpreting/translation. The graduate should be able to identify minority groups within the Deaf communities they serve, and appreciate that there may be cultural and linguistic diversity that are relevant to some of the subgroups that do not present in others.*

## Learning outcomes:

On successful completion of the course, graduates should be able to:

1. Critically evaluate sociological perspectives and theories of health and disability.

2. Describe what it means to be a member of a Deaf community.

## Deaf communities and Deaf Culture

3. Explain the connection between the development of language and identity.

4. Reflect on various definitions of Deaf communities.

5. Describe the kinds of discrimination and oppressive behaviours (including Audism) that impinge on Deaf individuals and/or communities.

6. Describe the historical context that notions of deafness, Deaf communities and Deafhood are grounded within.

7. Identify and describe the major milestones in Deaf history (including establishment of Deaf education, formation of communities, the 'Golden era' of manualism, the rise of oralism, the Congress of Milan 1880, the introduction of oral education and consequences thereof).

8. Describe the major philosophical influences on responses to deafness (give a detailed account of legal, religious, educational, rehabilitation, normalisation, eugenics, human rights, socio-cultural views and medical responses to deafness).

9. Outline the main causes of deafness, the classification of different types of hearing loss, the diagnosis of deafness and the consequences of impaired hearing.

## Deaf communities and Deaf Culture

10. Describe the main characteristics of the education of Deaf people throughout history.

11. Summarise the prototypical traditions associated with Deaf communities (such as contemporary Deaf folklore).

12. Compare and contrast language transmission pathways for deaf people born into Deaf or hearing families, and the consequences of same.

13. Identify and describe minority groups within a Deaf community (such as Deaf people with disabilities, Deafblind people, Deaf gay/lesbians, Deaf people who are members of minority religious communities, and/or Deaf people who are members of ethnic minority populations).

14. List and describe knowledge of the key global, European, national, and local organisations for Deaf and hard of hearing people.

15. Justify the importance of the move to preserve and protect Deaf Culture and Deaf heritage.

# Ethics and Decision Making

*Domain of knowledge 5*

## Summary goal:

*A graduate should demonstrate the capacity to apply professional, ethical decision making in a manner consistent with professional standards in terms of linguistic and interpersonal decision making. They should critically appraise the national/institutional Codes of Ethics/Practice and have a clear sense of how their personal values align or conflict with Deaf community values, or those espoused by the interpreting profession. A graduate should be able to explain the scope of practice of a sign language interpreter to consumers. Graduates should employ professional behaviours in all of their dealings with consumers and colleagues.*

## Learning outcomes:

On successful completion of the course, graduates should be able to:

1. Describe and justify one's own set of values and evaluate how these may conflict with Codes of Ethics/Practice and Deaf community values.

## ethics and decision making

2. Recall and critically evaluate the standards of professional responsibility, conduct and behaviours entailed within Codes of Ethics/Practice.

3. Demonstrate critical reflection and decision-making skills relative to specific ethical/professional dilemmas taking into account appropriate protocols for the environment.

4. Describe the historical evolution of the interpreter's role.

5. Compare and contrast the role of the interpreter in different interpreting settings (such as educational, conference, legal, medical, interpreting for Deafblind people, interpreting for children).

6. Describe decision-making process strategies and models for interpreters.

7. Critically discuss potential choices and impacts arising when dealing with an ethical/professional dilemma in an interpreting situation.

8. Apply professional, ethical decision-making in a manner consistent with professional standards in terms of linguistic and interpersonal decision-making.

# Interpreting for Specific Populations

*Domain of knowledge 6*

## Summary goal:

*A graduate should demonstrate capacity to work effectively and efficiently with members of a specified population (e.g. Deafblind, deafened adults, consumers with minimal language competence, cochlear implant clients and hard of hearing persons), using appropriate interpreting modes, and operating as a fully contributing member of an interpreting team. They should be familiar with the range of technologies used by members of a specific population, and flexible in their scope of practice, recognising that they may also be called on to function outside the typically expected interpreting role (e.g. when working as Deafblind guides).*

## Learning outcomes:

On successful completion of the course, graduates should be able to:

1. Describe the main characteristics of the relevant specific population (e.g. Deafblind, deafened adults, consumers with minimal language competence, CI-clients and hard of hearing persons).

*interpreting for specific populations*

2. Describe the technologies used by the relevant specific population.

3. Consult effectively with consumers to determine their individual needs and integrate these preferences as appropriate.

4. Interpret in consecutive and simultaneous modes.

5. Explain the rationale behind the interpreting mode selected.

6. Work as part of a relay team.

The following are learning outcomes specified for key specific populations:

### Deafblind people:

7. Describe types of visions loss and various etiologies.

8. Describe the causes and types of deafblindness, the range of communication systems used and environmental adaptations required.

9. Describe different methods of tactile communication employed by Deafblind people.

## *interpreting for specific populations*

10. Demonstrate guiding and environmental description techniques.

11. Demonstrate capacity to negotiate and monitor use of modified signing space and pace of signing for people with reduced visual field.

12. Participate as a Deafblind interpreter in Deafblind group meetings.

### *Deafened adults:*

13. Describe types of hearing loss and their common causes.

14. Explain the characteristics of deafened populations from a psychological and sociological perspective.

### *Consumers with minimal language competences:*

15. Describe the common features of language restriction typically presented by individuals with minimal language competency.

16. Demonstrate techniques for working in an interpreting team with Deaf and hearing interpreters.

## *interpreting for specific populations*

### *Persons with Cochlear Impant(s) and hard of hearing persons:*

17. Produce and comprehend sign supported language to present clear, detailed descriptions on a wide range of subjects commensurate with B2 level (CEFR).

# Interpreting in Specific Settings

*Domain of knowledge 7*

## Prologue:

Interpreting in specific settings in this document means interpreting in health care settings, educational settings, employment settings, institutional settings (including formal religious settings) and interpreting in social settings (including sporting and artistic settings, etc.). Interpreter training programmes should expand the definition of these particular settings at local level.

## Summary goal:

*A graduate should demonstrate a specified threshold of competency relevant to interpreting in the specialised domain. They should demonstrate an understanding of the characteristics of the specific domain and adapt their professional behaviour and practice to this specific context in terms of following protocol, integrating discourse norms, terminology and professional practices. They demonstrate capacity as reflective practitioners who work technically in their relevant specialised domain, and are committed to ongoing professional development.*

*interpreting in specific settings*

## Learning outcomes:

On successful completion of the course, graduates should be able to:

1. Outline the key settings for the relevant specialised domain that the graduate will work within.

2. Describe the normative scope of practice for an interpreter working in the relevant specialised domain.

3. Explain the scope of practice of other professionals working in the relevant specialised domain whom the interpreter will work alongside.

4. Integrate appropriate use of appropriate domain vocabulary in interpretation work.

5. Generate a working glossary of terms/concepts for the specialised interpreting domain.

6. Demonstrate capacity to apply Demand and Control Schema to the relevant specialised domain.

7. Critically appraise the key literature from the relevant specialised interpreting domain.

8. Summarise the most common professional/ethical challenges that may arise for interpreters in the relevant specialised domain.

9. Demonstrate capacity to self-evaluate proficiency in the relevant specialised domain.

## *interpreting in specific settings*

10. Work effectively with another interpreter in the relevant specialised domain.

11. Work effectively with other professionals in the relevant specialised domain.

12. Generate interpretations that reflect the register and style of the consumers and the context.

13. Practise safely in the relevant specialised domain (health and safety considerations).

# Professional Knowledge

*Domain of knowledge 8*

## Summary goal:

> *A graduate should advocate for conditions of employment that safeguard the rights and welfare of consumers and interpreters, and demonstrate professional integrity by avoiding conflicts of interest, adhering to their local Code of Ethics/Practice, and applying standard professional business practices.*

## Learning outcomes:

On successful completion of the course, graduates should be able to:

1. Critically reflect on core aspects of translation studies (including historical and contemporary perspectives).

2. Describe the aims and objectives of their national/local interpreter/translation association.

3. Outline the key principles enshrined in legal acts regulating sign language interpreting services, if applicable.

4. Demonstrate the know-how associated with maintaining a healthy musculoskeletal system.

## professional knowledge

5. Describe local business practices for freelance practitioners (invoicing, legislation, tax obligations, VAT, etc.).

6. Prepare a professional portfolio and documents relevant for job application processes (curriculum vitae, covering letter, etc.).

7. Demonstrate capacity to apply the key tenets of their local Code of Ethics/Practice.

8. Identify and describe differences in scope of practice that apply to interpreters as employees versus interpreters as freelance practitioners.

9. Apply domain-specific protocols to interpreting practice.

# Glossary

*Audism:*

1. Audism is a term to describe discrimination or stereotypes of deaf or hard of hearing people, for example by assuming that the cultural ways of hearing people are preferable or superior to those of deaf or signing culture, or that deaf people are somehow less capable than hearing people. (Source: http://www.deaflinx.com/DeafCommunity/audism.html)

2. The notion that one is superior based on one's ability to hear or behave in the manner of one who hears. (Tom Humphrey 1977, quoted in Zak 1996)

3. An attitude based on pathological thinking which results in a negative stigma toward anyone who does not hear; like racism or sexism, audism judges, labels, and limits individuals on the basis of whether a person hears and speaks. (Humphrey and Alcorn 1995: 85)

4. The belief that life without hearing is futile and miserable, that hearing loss is a tragedy and "the scourge of mankind," and that deaf people should struggle to be as much like hearing people as possible. Audists, hearing or deaf, shun Deaf culture and the use of sign language, and have what Reed and Teuber describe as "an obsession with the use of residual hearing, speech, and lipreading by deaf people." (Pelka 1997: 33)

5. The corporate institution for dealing with deaf people--dealing with them by making statements about them, au-

*glossary*

thorizing views of them, describing them, teaching about them, governing where they go to school and, in some cases, where they live; in short, audism is the hearing way of dominating, restructuring, and exercising authority over the deaf community. It includes such professional people as administrators of schools for deaf children and of training programs for deaf adults, interpreters, and some audiologists, speech therapists, otologists, psychologists, psychiatrists, librarians, researchers, social workers, and hearing aid specialists. (Lane 1992: 43)

## *Consecutive interpreting:*

The process of interpreting after the speaker or signer has completed one or more ideas in the source language and pauses whilst the interpreter transmits that information (Russell 2005: 136). See also Simultaneous Interpreting.

## *Continuous Professional Development (profile and plan):*

The notion of continuing to undertake tasks, engage in activities and personal study which will contribute to the ongoing development of knowledge and skills thus enhancing professional practice.

*glossary*

A *profile* is a statement details the current status and development needs of the professional.

A *plan* is a detailed proposal of what tasks and activities the professional will undertake over a specified period of time.

*Deafhood:*

Deafhood is not seen as a finite state but as a process "the struggle by each Deaf child, Deaf family and Deaf adult to explain to themselves and each other their own existence in the world" (Ladd 2003: 3). He suggests that through Deafhood, Deaf individuals come to actualise their Deaf identity.

*Demand and Control Schema:*

1. A model for effective interpretation that considers the challenges of a job (demands) and what resources are available to respond to a demand (controls).

2. Dean and Pollard (2001) adapted the demand control concept from occupational research conducted by Robert Karasek (1979) and Törres Theorell (Karasek & Theorell, 1990) who recognised that occupational stress and illness, or work satisfaction and effectiveness, arise from

*glossary*

an interactive dynamic between the challenges (demands) presented by work tasks in relation to the resources (controls or decision latitude) that workers bring to bear in response to job demands theory to examine the nature of demands and controls in the interpreting profession specifically. Dean and Pollard (2001) used the framework of D-C.

*Discourse Analysis:*

Discourse analysis is the act of distinguishing and considering the component parts of a message in order to understand the whole of the message. (Witter-Merithew, 1987). Discourse Analysis is used in examining "how humans use language to communicate and, in particular, how addressers construct linguistic messages for addressees and how addressees work on linguistic messages in order to interpret them." (Brown and Yule 1983).

*Discourse Mapping:*

Discourse mapping is based on discourse analysis. It is a technique that teaches students how to develop a mental picture of the meaning structure in any given text. By creating an actual map of a text, students can see the relationship of its three perspectives: content, context and form. It provides a systematic approach for teaching students to analyse a text so that they can produce successful, effective interpretations which are accurate in content, socially appropriate and linguistically accurate. (Winston and Monikowski 2000).

## *Efforts model:*

A series of models for consecutive and simultaneous interpreting developed by Daniel Gile (1995). The implications of Gile's models are discussed for sign language interpreters in Leeson (2005).

## *Manualism / Manual approach:*

The practice of employing and promoting the use of a sign language as the primary means of communication in deaf education (Leeson 2006). See also Oralism.

## *Miscue Analysis:*

An approach developed by Cokely (1992) to identify types and frequency of miscues (i.e. additions, omissions, substitutions, intrusions and anomalies) in interpreted output.

*glossary*

*Oralism / oral education:*

> The promotion of lipreading, training in speech production and training of residual hearing as the primary means of communication in deaf educational settings. (Leeson 2006).

*Portfolio (professional):*

> A collection of documents, (e.g. loose papers, photographs, references, digital materials and other relevant documentation) which provide a professional profile and showcase experience and expertise.

*Relay interpreting :*

> Relay interpreting refers to contexts where an interpreted message is relayed via a chain of interpreters because no one common source language is known by all interpreters on the interpreting team. For example, French could be a source language at a conference and then this is interpreted to English, with interpreters working from the English to relay the message into a range of other languages. Relay interpreting in this sense occurs in both signed and spoken language contexts. The European Commission describes this as "interpreting between two languages via a third". (http://ec.europa.eu/

*glossary*

dgs/scic/what-is-conference-interpreting/)

*Remote interpreting:*

This refers to a communicative situation in which all primary participants are at a single location, whilst the interpreter is at another (remote) location and linked to the primary participants via videoconference. See also Videoconference Interpreting. (http://www.videoconference-interpreting.net)

*Sight interpreting / sight translation:*

"Sight translation can be defined as the reading of a text by the interpreter from the source language into the target language, simultaneously, in a manner in which the content of the document can be easily understood by the audience." (http://linkterpreting.uvigo.es/que-es-la-interpretacion/tecnicas/simultanea/traduccion-a-vista/?lang=en)

*Sign supported language / manually coded language:*

In a particular country, a manual code representing the morphemes of the dominant language may be used. In deaf education, teachers sometimes use such a manually coded form of the national/regional spoken language while they simultaneously speak the message they are signing (Baker and Knight 1998).

## *Simultaneous interpreting:*

The process of interpreting into the target language at the same time as the source language is being delivered. (Russell 2005) See also Consecutive Interpreting.

## *Skopos Theory:*

This is an approach to translation developed by Vermeer (1978). "Skopos" is derived from the Greek and is used as a technical term for the purpose, aim, goal or objective of a translation. Skopos must be defined before translation can begin: in highlighting skopos, the theory adopts a prospective attitude to translation, as opposed to a retrospective attitude adopted in theories which focus on prescriptions derived from the source text" (Schaffner 2009:117)

*glossary*

*Tactile Sign Language:*

>Tactile sign language is used primarily by Deafblind people who, experience sign language in communicative settings by holding the hands of their conversational partner and feeling the hand movements. Mesch (2001) describes how Deaf people who have some visual ability left still use the visual-gesture conversational form despite their limited vision. These people can compensate by using the tactile conversational form, for instance, when the lighting is bad. For completely blind people, tactile sign language is the only conversational form. This is often the case for people whose vision gradually deteriorates, that is, whose field of vision slowly narrows, so that the method of reading changes little by little from the visual to the tactile form.

*Text:*

>Text for the purposes of this document refers to any part, parts or whole of a message that is either written, spoken or signed.

*Threshold level of pass*:

>The minimum standard required for a pass grade.

*glossary*

---

*Videoconference interpreting:*
> This is where an interpreter is involved in a communicative situation where the primary participants are at two or more different locations that are linked via videoconference. The interpreter is located with one of the primary participants.

# glossary

*Tactile Sign Language:*

> Tactile sign language is used primarily by Deafblind people who, experience sign language in communicative settings by holding the hands of their conversational partner and feeling the hand movements. Mesch (2001) describes how Deaf people who have some visual ability left still use the visual-gesture conversational form despite their limited vision. These people can compensate by using the tactile conversational form, for instance, when the lighting is bad. For completely blind people, tactile sign language is the only conversational form. This is often the case for people whose vision gradually deteriorates, that is, whose field of vision slowly narrows, so that the method of reading changes little by little from the visual to the tactile form.

*Text:*

> Text for the purposes of this document refers to any part, parts or whole of a message that is either written, spoken or signed.

*Threshold level of pass*:

> The minimum standard required for a pass grade.

*glossary*

*Videoconference interpreting:*
> This is where an interpreter is involved in a communicative situation where the primary participants are at two or more different locations that are linked via videoconference. The interpreter is located with one of the primary participants.

# References

- Baker, Rob and Pamela Knight 1998: 'Total Communication' – current policy and practice. In Gregory, Susan; Pamela Knight, Wendy McCracken, Stephen Powers and Linda Watson (eds.): Issues in Deaf Education. London: David Fulton, 77-88.

- Brown, Gillian and George Yule 1983: Discourse Analysis. Cambridge: Cambridge University Press.

- Calle Alberdi, Lourdes 2013: Sign Language Interpreter Training Programmes. European Forum of Sign Language Interpreters report 2011, updated in 2012 and 2013.

- Cokely, Dennis 1992: Miscue Analysis. Burtonsville, Md.:Linstok Press.

- Dean, Robyn and Pollard, Robert Q. 2001: Application of Demand-Control Theory to Sign Interpreter Training: Implications for Stress and Interpreter Training. Journal of Deaf Studies and Deaf Education. 6 (1) 1-14.

- Gile, Daniel 1995: Basic concepts and models for interpreter and translator training. Amsterdam: John Benjamins.

- Leeson, Lorraine 2005: Making the Effort in Simultaneous Interpreting: Some considerations for signed language interpreters. In Terry Janzen (ed.) Topics in Signed Language Interpreting. Amsterdam and Philadelphia: John Benjamins.

# references

51-68.

- Leeson, Lorraine 2006: Signed Languages in Education in Europe – a preliminary exploration. Strasbourg: Council of Europe. Council of Europe Language Policy Division.

- Ladd, Paddy 2003: Understanding deaf culture : in search of deafhood. Clevedon: Multilingual Matters.

- Mesch, Johanna 2001: Tactile Sign Language: Turn taking and Questions in Signed Conversations of Deaf-Blind People. Hamburg: Signum Verlag.

- Russell, Debra 2005: Consecutive and Simultaneous Interpreting. In Terry Janzen (ed.) Topics in Sign Language Interpreting. Amsterdam and Philadelphia: John Benjamins.

- Shaffner, Christine 2009: Functionalist Approaches. In Mona Baker and Gabriela Saldanha (eds.) Routledge encyclopedia of translation studies. London: Routeledge. 115-121

- Van den Bogaerde, Beppie and Oyserman, Joni 2011: Implementing CEFR in the Curriculum for Sign Language of the Netherlands (NGT). Paper presented at ESF Workshop on CEFR and Sign Language Curricula. Zürich, Switzerland, September 2011.

- Winston, Elizabeth and Christine Monikowsi 2000: Dis-

*references*

---

course Mapping: Developing textual coherence skills in interpreters. In Cynthia Roy (ed.) Innovative Practices for Teaching Sign Language Interpreters. Washington DC: Gallaudet University Press. 15-59.

- Witter-Merithew, A. 1987: Text analysis. In M. L. McIntire (ed.), New Dimensions in Interpreter Education: Curriculum & instruction. Proceedings of the sixth national Conference of Interpreter Trainers convention. Chevy Chase, MD: Registry of Interpreters for the Deaf. 77-82.

## Websites

- European Commission DG Interpreting: http://ec.europa.eu/dgs/scic/what-is-conference-interpreting/ (accessed 23 July 2013)

- Demand and Control Schema: http://www.urmc.rochester.edu/deaf-wellness-center/demand-control-schema/overview.cfm (accessed 23 July 2013)

- Distance Opportunities for Interpreter Training Center, *Entry-to-Practice competencies for ASL/English interpreters*: http://www.unco.edu/doit/Competencies_brochure_handout.pdf (accessed 8 August 2013)

*references*

- National Council on Interpreting in Health Care: http://www.ncihc.org/ (accessed 8 August 2013)

- Universidade de Vigo "Linkterpreting" Site: http://linkterpreting.uvigo.es/que-es-la-interpretacion/tecnicas/simultanea/traduccion-a-vista/?lang=en (accessed 23 July 2013)

- Videoconference and Remote Interpreting: http://www.videoconference-interpreting.net (accessed 23 July 2013)

www.ingramcontent.com/pod-product-compliance
Lightning Source LLC
Chambersburg PA
CBHW021813220426
43662CB00006B/300